Chef Freddie
and Friends

Cooking Under the
Rainbow

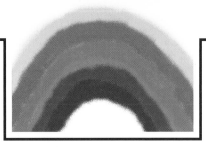

Cooking Under the Rainbow

Copyright © 2000

Lahey Clinic
41 Mall Road, Burlington, MA 01805-0105
781-744-8257

Library of Congress Number: 99-075518
ISBN: 0-9675729-0-8

Designed, Edited, and Manufactured by
Favorite Recipes® Press
an imprint of

FRP™

P.O. Box 305142, Nashville, Tennessee 37230
1-800-358-0560

Lahey Clinic Cookbook Director: Lisa G. Polacke
Book Concept and Implementation: Cathie and Donald Macrelli
Book Design: Jim Scott
Art Director: Steve Newman
Project Manager: Susan Larson

Manufactured in the United States of America
First Printing: 2000   5,000 copies

Black and white line art copyrighted by Linda Zebrowski

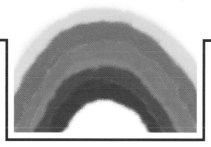

Dedication

Cooking Under the Rainbow *is a children's cookbook designed to bring parents and children together through food and fun. This cookbook is dedicated to David Ferdinand Macrelli and all the young children of the world. In creating this book, we hoped to capture and foster David's zest and spirit for life. Our children are the best investment in the future we can make.*
It is with this goal we write this book.

Cathleen and Donald Macrelli

No endeavor is ever accomplished alone, and no one can come through the pain of tragedy without family and friends to guide them. When our son David died unexpectedly in 1996 at the tender age of 18 months, we could not imagine the next day, let alone where we are today. Our hearts were so heavy with grief, and we never imagined that one could feel such agony.

Many people put aside their own personal lives and problems to call us, comfort us, send cards and even cook for us. There are also those who cried with us, and some who simply listened when we so desperately needed to talk. We never felt like we were alone, and for this we are eternally grateful.

As the months grow into years, there are new people who meet us, and through us they meet David and learn about David's Fund. They are helping us to go forward into tomorrow, and to make sure that little David Macrelli is not forgotten. We will miss David forever and our hearts still ache — he would have loved this book.

Donald J. Macrelli

David's Fund

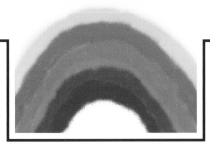

Introduction

The cooking area of our homes has always been a place of gathering, where children are educated in many aspects of life. Children are in the kitchen through all of their growing years.

In infancy, they sit in their little seats watching mommy or daddy prepare meals. As toddlers, their earliest words can be "juice" or "cookies." As children grow, they love to create, and cooking is a natural creative playground.

Teaching reading and math can come from using recipes. Holiday food preparations make great memories for children. And the adolescent's focus on eating is not a myth! A healthy and fun recipe book for children and their nutrition is a natural addition to a full-service pediatrics program.

The Lahey Clinic's Department of Pediatrics and Adolescent Medicine embraces a philosophy of caring for the special needs of children and adolescents through health education, anticipatory guidance, and prevention. We try to reach out to our young patients, their families, and our employees through school projects, special events, and parental support.

The proceeds from this cookbook will support our ongoing projects and excellence in pediatrics at Lahey Clinic.

Claire D. Wilson, M.D.
Chair, Department of Pediatrics and Adolescent Medicine
Lahey Clinic Medical Center
Burlington, Massachusetts

Mission Statement

David's Fund was established in 1996 in memory of David F. Macrelli, son of Cathleen and Donald Macrelli. Its purpose is to foster excellence in child care at Lahey Clinic.

The income from David's Fund will enhance pediatric services by supporting nursing education, parental counseling and education, and the purchase of educational toys and equipment in the Clinic's Pediatric Department. The Fund will also benefit expanded services at a proposed day care center. Through David's Fund, families and children will be enriched, and children will be given the finest possible care at Lahey Clinic.

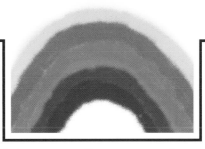

Acknowledgements

It is with fond remembrance that we acknowledge the following people for going beyond the expected, and helping us in ways they may not have even realized were so meaningful.

Darryll Baker
Dr. Paul Cammarata
Maria Centola
Teri Frates
Dennis Goodwin
Patty Goodwin
Janet Habeshian
Linda Haynes
Mike Hugo
John Libertino, M.D.
Jennifer Lipman, M.D.
James Lopez
Francesco Lunardi
Judy MacLellan
Bob Macrelli
Ed Macrelli
Marie "Dolly" Macrelli
Ed McGee
Prof. Peter Meyers
Rich Miner
Paul O'Connor

Lou Pasquale
Patty Pasquale
Carl Peterson
Chris Peterson
Kim Peterson
Mary Peterson
Mary Pat Peterson
Sharon Peterson
Lisa Polacke

Patricia Roberts, M.D.
Michelle Rosa
Cheryl Schiefer
The Staff of 7 Central
Andrew Vega
Buffi Vega
Gene Vega
Christine Ward
Shannon Weisse

Donald, Cathie, and David Macrelli

A special thank you to David's cousins: Robert, Elena, Hillary, Matthew, Sarah, and Ethan. It is from the mouths of babes that our hearts are warmed the most. We hope that they will grow up to realize that their innocent words and actions have kept us afloat, and keep us hopeful that David's spirit will be kept alive.

Kitchens Teach Kids About Food, Love, and Life

When I was growing up, the kitchen was the heartbeat of our home. Everything that was wonderful and warm originated from this room. Family gatherings, tender moments, minor accidents, and sometimes major conflicts were all natural and resolved in this haven. But the best part, the part that kept all the family, friends, and neighbors returning, was the warmth of its food. To me, my mother was Julia Child, June Cleaver, and my Mom all rolled into one.

From a very young age I remember my mother getting us involved in helping her prepare meals, and never once do I remember distress about the mess. That was never the point. The final product, and the fun in getting there, was always what was important. And best of all, I felt that I had created something wonderful to share with the people I loved. I felt a sense of accomplishment.

I also learned the value of tradition. Making "Grandma's Irish Bread" felt worldly to me. Like something that was historical and needed to be treasured. But more importantly, I learned good nutrition and good cooking. Food was life!

These feelings have been with me all of my life. When our son David was born, my husband Donald (who also learned the value of tradition) and I naturally made our kitchen a haven too. It served warmth, laughter, tender moments, and lots of messy creative meals. It was where we danced on Saturday nights to the "oldies" on the radio while whipping up our sustenance. It was the heartbeat of our home.

It is with all of these memories and emotions that this cookbook was created.

Make your kitchen come to life for your children and infuse it with love. Children will never forget. Never underestimate the value of what can be created in your kitchen.

Contents

A Word About Allergies

Living with food allergies affects the whole family deeply. It has great emotional impact, probably more on the parents (or food preparer) than on the child. It can be difficult, time consuming, and scary to think that one taste, one molecule could be fatal.

Jacob, my son, is four years old and is severely allergic to dairy products, nuts, and eggs. This became a challenge that my husband and I adapted to, and thought was difficult, although there are more than enough food choices. It's almost like being a vegan who eats fish, turkey, and chicken. But now that he's older, and has more opportunities with food as a theme, it is difficult, but we manage. It presents to me the enjoyable, but time-consuming, task of cooking and baking wholesome meals and special treats. School is another challenge I will meet when the time comes around.

Scattered throughout this book are recipes and snacks that are fun and healthy for children with food allergies.

Located at the bottom of each recipe is a symbol bar similar to the one below. If the cow is colored, the recipe is milk protein free; if the chick is colored, the recipe is egg free; if the wheat is colored, the recipe is wheat free but not necessarily gluten or gliaden free; and if the nut is colored, the recipe is nut free. For instance, the symbol bar below would indicate that the recipe is milk protein free.

Prepackaged foods have not been analyzed to determine if the ingredients in them contain milk protein, eggs, wheat, or nuts. The responsibility for determining this lies with the individual preparing the recipe, or a responsible adult.

Carmen Goulet, D.C.

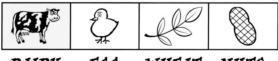

DAIRY   EGG   WHEAT   NUTS

GET UP AND GO

Ally, the cat

Breakfast & Snacks

Moonstruck Eggs

4 slices white bread
1 tablespoon olive oil
4 eggs
Salt and pepper to taste
Chopped parsley to taste
Grated Romano cheese to taste

Toast the bread until light brown. Cut a hole about the size of an egg in the center of each piece of toast.

Heat a nonstick skillet over medium-low heat. Coat the skillet with the olive oil.

Place the toast in the skillet. Break the eggs carefully into the holes in the toast. Cook until the eggs are of the desired firmness.

Sprinkle with salt, pepper, parsley and cheese.

Yield: 2 to 4 servings

Scrambled Eggs

8 eggs
Seasoned salt to taste
1/8 teaspoon baking soda
1/4 cup milk
2 tablespoons (1/4 stick) butter

Break the eggs into a bowl.

Add seasoned salt, baking soda and milk. Beat with a whisk until smooth.

Melt the butter in a large skillet over medium-low heat. Pour in the egg mixture.

Cook until of the desired firmness, stirring occasionally.

Serve with bacon and biscuits or toast.

Yield: 4 servings

Ally's
Easy Quiche

12 eggs
16 ounces Cheddar cheese, shredded
16 ounces Monterey Jack
cheese, shredded
1 cup salsa

Combine the eggs, Cheddar cheese,
Monterey Jack cheese and salsa
in a bowl and mix well. Pour into
a 9x11-inch baking dish.

Bake at 350 degrees for 35 to
40 minutes or until set in the center.

Yield: 12 servings

Did You Know...
That the word egghead dates back to the
1952 presidential campaign? It was
used to mean an intellectual with a high brow
and a head shaped like an egg, such as
Adlai Stevenson.

Irish Bread

4 cups flour
4 teaspoons baking powder
1 cup sugar
½ teaspoon salt
1½ cups raisins
½ cup (1 stick) butter
2 eggs, beaten
1 cup milk

Sift the flour, baking powder, sugar and salt into a bowl.

Combine a small amount of the flour mixture with the raisins in a bowl and toss to coat.

Cut the butter into the remaining flour mixture until crumbly. Add the eggs and milk and mix well. Stir in the raisins.

Shape into a loaf. Place in a greased and floured loaf pan. Sprinkle a small amount of flour over the top.

Bake at 350 degrees for 1 hour or until a knife inserted in the center comes out clean.

Yield: 12 servings

DID YOU KNOW...
THAT GOLDEN RAISINS AND DARK RAISINS ARE GRAPES THAT HAVE BEEN DRIED BY ARTIFICIAL HEAT OR BY THE SUN? APPROXIMATELY 50 PERCENT OF ALL RAISINS COME FROM CALIFORNIA.

Banana Bread

1 tablespoon Ener-G Egg Replacer
$\frac{1}{4}$ cup water
1$\frac{1}{4}$ cups sugar
$\frac{1}{2}$ cup butter-flavor shortening
3 or 4 bananas, mashed
$\frac{1}{2}$ cup rice milk
1 teaspoon vanilla extract
2$\frac{1}{2}$ cups flour
1 teaspoon baking soda
1 teaspoon salt

Grease the bottom of a 5x9-inch loaf pan.

Combine the Ener-G Egg Replacer and the water in a bowl and mix well.

Cream the sugar and shortening in a mixer bowl until light and fluffy. Beat in the Ener-G Egg Replacer mixture. Add the bananas, rice milk and vanilla and beat until smooth.

Add the flour, baking soda and salt, mixing just until moistened. Pour into the prepared pan.

Bake at 350 degrees on the lowest oven rack for 1$\frac{1}{4}$ hours or until a wooden pick inserted in the center comes out clean.

Yield: 12 servings

DID YOU KNOW...
THAT UNLIKE MOST OTHER FRUITS, BANANAS DEVELOP BETTER FLAVOR WHEN RIPENED OFF THE STEM? THE MORE YELLOW THE SKIN THE SWEETER THE FRUIT.

Bran Muffins

1¼ cups whole wheat flour
½ cup sugar
½ teaspoon salt
1 tablespoon baking powder
2 cups All-Bran extra-fiber cereal
1¼ cups milk
1 egg or 2 egg whites
¼ cup applesauce
1 apple, grated (optional)

Sift the flour, sugar, salt and baking powder into a bowl. Combine the cereal and milk in a separate bowl. Pour into the flour mixture and mix well. Add the egg, applesauce and apple and mix well.

Fill muffin cups sprayed with nonstick cooking spray ⅔ full. Bake at 400 degrees for 20 minutes.

Yield: 12 servings

Peanut Butter Muffins

2 cups flour
1 tablespoon baking powder
¼ teaspoon salt
1 egg
1½ cups milk
½ cup chunky peanut butter
½ cup packed light brown sugar
¼ cup vegetable oil
1 cup bran cereal
2 cups chopped bananas

Sift the flour, baking powder and salt together.

Combine the egg, milk, peanut butter, brown sugar and oil in a bowl and mix well. Stir in the bran cereal. Let stand for 5 minutes. Add the bananas and dry ingredients, stirring just until moistened. Fill muffin cups ⅔ full.

Bake at 400 degrees for 20 minutes or until golden brown. Cool in the pan on a wire rack.

Yield: 16 muffins

Cheddar Cheese Muffins with Apple Butter

2 cups flour
1/2 cup sugar
1 tablespoon baking powder
1/2 teaspoon salt
1/2 teaspoon baking soda
2 cups grated Cheddar cheese
1 cup plain yogurt
1/4 cup (1/2 stick) melted margarine
2 eggs, beaten
Apple Butter

Line large muffin cups with paper liners or grease the cups.

Mix the flour, sugar, baking powder, salt and baking soda in a bowl with a fork. Stir in the cheese gradually until evenly mixed. Make a well in the center of the mixture.

Whisk the yogurt, melted margarine and eggs in a small bowl. Add to the dry ingredients, stirring just until moistened; the batter will be very thick. Fill the prepared muffin cups 2/3 full. Bake at 400 degrees in the center of the oven for 18 to 20 minutes or until golden brown. Serve with Apple Butter.

Yield: 12 muffins

Apple Butter

1/2 cup (1 stick) butter, softened
1/2 cup apple jelly
1/4 teaspoon cinnamon

Beat the butter in a mixer bowl until creamy. Beat in the jelly and cinnamon until well blended.

Yield: 1 cup

Heath Brunch Coffee Cake

½ cup (1 stick) butter or margarine
1 cup packed light brown sugar
2 cups flour
½ cup sugar
1 cup buttermilk
1 egg
1 teaspoon baking soda
1 teaspoon vanilla extract
6 Heath bars, crushed
¼ cup chopped walnuts or pecans

Combine the butter, brown sugar, flour and sugar in a bowl and mix well. Reserve ½ cup of the mixture.

Add the buttermilk, egg, baking soda and vanilla to the remaining flour mixture and mix well. Pour into a greased and floured 9x13-inch baking pan.

Combine the reserved flour mixture, crushed Heath bars and walnuts in a bowl and mix well. Sprinkle over the batter. Bake at 350 degrees for 30 minutes or until a wooden pick inserted in the center comes out clean.

Yield: 12 to 15 servings

DID YOU KNOW...
THAT GEORGIA PRODUCES APPROXIMATELY
130 MILLION POUNDS OF PECANS A YEAR? THE
WORD PECAN IS DERIVED FROM THE WORD
PACCAN, AN ALGONQUIAN WORD MEANING
"NUT WITH A HARD SHELL TO CRACK."

Overnight Coffee Cake

1 package frozen cloverleaf roll dough
¹/₂ cup (1 stick) melted
butter or margarine
¹/₂ cup packed light brown sugar
1 (4-ounce) package vanilla
instant pudding mix
¹/₂ cup chopped pecans

Separate each roll into 3 pieces. Place in a buttered bundt pan. Pour the melted butter over the dough.

Combine the brown sugar, pudding mix and pecans in a bowl and mix well. Sprinkle over the buttered dough. Let stand, covered, to rise overnight.

Bake at 350 degrees for 20 to 30 minutes or until browned. Invert onto a serving plate.

Yield: 8 servings

DID YOU KNOW...
THAT BAKING SODA CAN BE USED TO REDUCE THE ITCH OF RASHES, POISON IVY, AND CHICKEN POX?

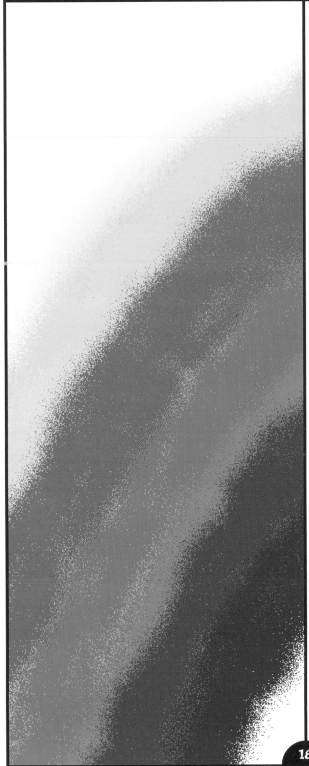

Pineapple Coffee Cake

1 (8-ounce) can crushed pineapple
1 egg
¼ cup sugar
2 cups Bisquick
Cinnamon to taste
Brown sugar to taste
Nutmeg to taste

Drain the pineapple, reserving ¾ cup juice. Combine the reserved juice, egg and sugar in a bowl and mix well. Add the Bisquick and mix well. Pour into a greased 9x9-inch baking pan.

Spread the drained pineapple over the batter. Sprinkle with cinnamon, brown sugar and nutmeg.

Bake at 350 degrees for 20 minutes or until a wooden pick inserted in the center comes out clean.

Yield: 9 servings

Ally-Oop Pancakes

1½ teaspoons Ener-G Egg Replacer
1 cup flour
¾ cup (or more) rice milk
1 tablespoon brown sugar
1½ tablespoons vegetable oil
1 tablespoon baking powder
¼ teaspoon salt

Combine the Ener-G Egg Replacer, flour, rice milk, brown sugar, oil, baking powder and salt in a bowl and mix until smooth. Add additional milk for a thinner batter.

Pour ¼ cup at a time onto a hot lightly greased griddle. Bake over medium heat until bubbles appear on the surface and the underside is golden brown. Turn the pancake over. Bake until golden brown.

Yield: 12 pancakes

Freckle-Faced Pancakes

1 banana
2 cups Bisquick
2 eggs
1 cup plain yogurt
½ teaspoon cinnamon
½ cup chocolate chips or raisins

Mash the banana in a bowl. Add the Bisquick, eggs, yogurt and cinnamon and mix well. Fold in the chocolate chips.

Pour ¼ cup at a time onto a hot griddle sprayed with nonstick cooking spray. Bake until bubbles appear on the surface and the underside is golden brown. Turn the pancake over. Bake until golden brown.

Yield: 24 pancakes

DID YOU KNOW...
THAT SPANISH MOSS IS A MEMBER OF THE PINEAPPLE FAMILY? POPULARLY BELIEVED TO BE A PARASITE THAT CHOKES A TREE, IT IS NEITHER A PARASITE NOR DOES IT HARM TREES.

Fluffy Waffles

1 cup self-rising flour
2 teaspoons sugar
³/₄ cup milk
2 eggs
2 teaspoons vegetable oil

Combine the flour and sugar in a bowl. Stir in the milk, eggs and oil, blending well.

Bake ¹/₂ cup at a time on a hot waffle iron sprayed with nonstick cooking spray until golden brown.

Yield: 3 waffles

Ally's Quick Breakfast

2 slices bread, toasted
2 tablespoons crunchy peanut butter
1 banana
Honey
Crisp rice cereal

Spread the hot toast with the peanut butter.

Slice the banana lengthwise and then into halves crosswise. Place 2 pieces of the banana on each piece of toast.

Drizzle honey over the banana. Sprinkle with cereal.

Yield: 2 servings

Crunchy French Toast

2 eggs
1/2 cup milk
1/2 teaspoon cinnamon
2 tablespoons vegetable oil
2 cups cornflakes
6 slices white bread
Butter
Maple syrup

Beat the eggs in a bowl until well mixed. Add the milk and cinnamon and mix well.

Heat the oil in a skillet over medium heat.

Place the cornflakes on a flat plate. Dip the bread slices in the egg mixture, coating both sides. Dip in the cornflakes, coating both sides.

Place in the hot skillet. Bake until brown on both sides.

Serve with butter and maple syrup.

Yield: 6 servings

Banana Smunchies

4 bananas, mashed
2 cups peanut butter
52 graham cracker squares

Combine the bananas and peanut butter in a bowl and mix well. Chill, covered, for 8 to 12 hours.

Spread 2 tablespoons of the peanut butter mixture over each graham cracker square. Cover half the squares with a second square peanut butter sides together. Wrap individually in foil.

Freeze for several hours.

Yield: 26 smunchies

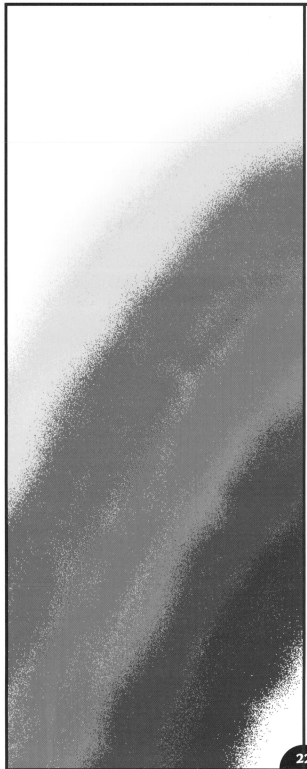

Millet with Cinnamon and Spices

3 cups water
$\frac{1}{2}$ cup millet
$\frac{1}{2}$ cup rolled oats
$\frac{1}{3}$ cup unsalted sunflower kernels
$\frac{1}{3}$ cup raisins
1 teaspoon vanilla extract
$\frac{1}{4}$ teaspoon cinnamon
$\frac{1}{2}$ cup toasted wheat germ

Bring the water to a boil over high heat. Reduce the heat to medium.

Add the millet, oats, sunflower kernels, raisins, vanilla and cinnamon and mix well. Simmer for 15 to 20 minutes or until all the water is absorbed. Sprinkle the wheat germ over the top.

Serve hot or cold with soy or rice milk.

Yield: 2 servings

DID YOU KNOW...
THAT MILLET IS THOUGHT TO BE ONE OF THE FIRST CROPS EVER CULTIVATED, POSSIBLY AS LONG AS 5000 YEARS AGO?

Cream of Barley with Oats

*3 cups water
2 cups quick-cooking barley
1 cup rolled oats
1 banana, sliced
1 teaspoon vanilla extract*

Bring the water to a boil in a saucepan over high heat. Reduce the heat to medium. Add the barley, whisking constantly. Add the oats, banana and vanilla and mix well.

Cook for 12 to 15 minutes.

Serve hot or cold with soy or rice milk.

Yield: 2 servings

Cream of Barley with Quinoa

*3 cups water
2 cups quick-cooking barley
1 cup quinoa
1 banana, sliced
1 teaspoon almond or vanilla extract
1/2 cup chopped dates or raisins*

Bring the water to a boil in a medium saucepan over high heat. Reduce the heat to medium.

Add the barley, whisking constantly. Stir in the quinoa, banana, almond extract and dates.

Cook for 12 to 15 minutes.

Serve hot or cold with soy or rice milk.

Yield: 2 servings

Blender Breakfast

1 banana
2 cups cold milk
2 scoops any flavor ice cream
¼ cup Ovaltine

Combine the banana, milk, ice cream and Ovaltine in a blender container. Process until smooth.

Yield: 2 servings

Fruit Smoothies

2 cups fat-free vanilla yogurt
4 to 6 ice cubes
Any combination of the following:
½ cup blueberries
1 peach or nectarine, chopped
1 mango, chopped
1 banana, sliced

Combine the yogurt, ice cubes and fruit in a blender container. Process until smooth and creamy. Pour into glasses and serve immediately.

Yield: 2 servings

DID YOU KNOW...
THAT DANNON IS THE AMERICAN VERSION OF DANONE? THE COMPANY, FOUNDED IN BARCELONA BY ISAAC CARASSO AND NAMED FOR HIS SON DANONE (DANIEL), WAS THE FIRST COMMERCIAL YOGURT DAIRY. IT MOVED TO NEW YORK AFTER WORLD WAR II.

Microwave Apples

2 red apples
Sugar to taste
Cinnamon to taste

Peel the apples and cut into bite-size pieces.

Arrange the apple pieces on a microwave-safe plate. Sprinkle with sugar and cinnamon.

Microwave on High for 3 to 4 minutes. Sprinkle with sugar. Let stand until cooled.

Yield: 2 servings

Granola

5 cups rolled oats
1 cup wheat germ
1 cup shredded unsweetened coconut
1 cup sliced almonds
1 cup sunflower kernels
$1/2$ cup sesame seeds
$3/4$ cup vegetable oil
$3/4$ cup honey

Combine the oats, wheat germ, coconut, almonds, sunflower kernels and sesame seeds in a roasting pan and mix well.

Combine the oil and honey in a bowl and mix well. Pour over the oat mixture and mix well.

Bake at 325 degrees for 30 to 60 minutes or until light brown and dry, stirring every 15 minutes.

May be mixed with applesauce or yogurt, served with milk, or sprinkled over fruit, yogurt or ice cream.

Yield: $9^1/2$ cups

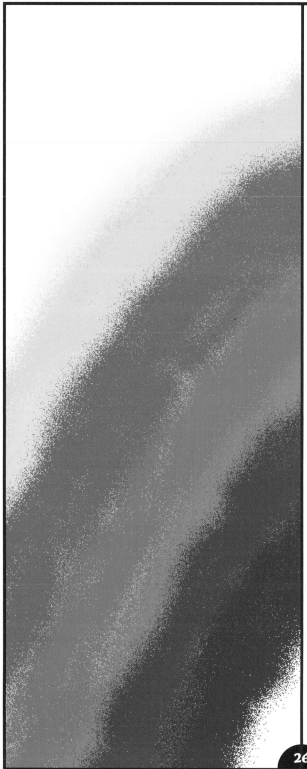

Rainbow
Pudding

*1 (4-ounce) package vanilla
instant pudding mix
2 cups cold milk
Red, blue, yellow and green
food coloring*

Combine the pudding mix and
milk in a bowl and mix until completely
smooth and slightly thickened.

Let stand for a few minutes until
completely thickened.

Divide the pudding into 4 bowls.

Add a drop of food coloring to each
bowl and mix well.

Refrigerate, covered, until
ready to serve.

Yield: 4 servings

TAKE A BREAK

Bonnie Bubbles

Lunch, Snacks & Crafts

Chicken Noodle Soup

1 (4-pound) chicken
12 cups water
1 tablespoon chicken bouillon granules
1$\frac{1}{2}$ teaspoons salt
$\frac{3}{4}$ teaspoon pepper
1$\frac{1}{2}$ teaspoons onion powder
$\frac{1}{4}$ teaspoon garlic powder
1 teaspoon seasoned salt
1 bay leaf
$\frac{1}{4}$ teaspoon celery salt
$\frac{1}{4}$ teaspoon basil
1 large green bell pepper, chopped
4 carrots, chopped
1 (8-ounce) package wide egg noodles
1$\frac{1}{2}$ cups milk

Place the chicken in a large stockpot. Add the water, bouillon granules, salt, pepper, onion powder, garlic powder, seasoned salt, bay leaf, celery salt and basil. Bring to a boil. Reduce the heat. Simmer for 1 hour or until the chicken is tender.

Remove the chicken, reserving the broth. Let stand to cool. Cut into bite-sized pieces, discarding the skin and bones. Set aside.

Add the green pepper and carrots to the reserved broth. Bring to a boil. Boil for 8 minutes.

Add the noodles. Cook until tender.

Add the cut-up chicken and milk. Simmer over low heat for 5 minutes. Remove the bay leaf.

Yield: 10 servings

Minestrone Soup

¼ cup chopped yellow or sweet onion
¼ cup chopped leeks
2 cups chopped tomatoes
¼ cup extra-virgin olive oil
3½ to 4 cups water
1½ cups chopped carrots
1 cup diced russet potatoes
2 garlic cloves, crushed
2 tablespoons chopped fresh parsley
2 tablespoons chopped fresh basil
1 bay leaf
1 teaspoon sea salt
1 teaspoon pepper
1 cup macaroni
½ cup chopped kale
1 cup cooked white beans
¼ cup chopped zucchini
¼ cup chopped parsnip or turnip

Sauté the onion, leeks and tomatoes in the olive oil in a skillet for 5 minutes.

Add the water and bring to a boil. Reduce the heat to medium. Add the carrots, potatoes, garlic, parsley, basil, bay leaf, ½ teaspoon of the salt and ½ teaspoon of the pepper.

Cook, partially covered, for 15 to 20 minutes. Add the macaroni, kale, beans, zucchini, parsnip, remaining ½ teaspoon salt and remaining ½ teaspoon pepper.

Cook over medium to high heat for 2½ to 3 hours. Remove the bay leaf. Serve with whole grain bread.

Yield: 2 to 4 servings

DID YOU KNOW...

THAT SOME PEOPLE BELIEVE THE PHRASE "SPILLING THE BEANS" CAME FROM THE GYPSIES, WHOSE FORTUNE-TELLERS USED TO PREDICT THE FUTURE FROM THE WAY A HANDFUL OF BEANS SPILLED OUT ON A FLAT SURFACE? OTHER PEOPLE BELIEVE THE PHRASE ORIGINATES FROM SECRET GREEK SOCIETIES WHOSE MEMBERS USED WHITE AND BLACK BEANS FOR VOTING ON THE ADMISSION OF NEW MEMBERS. IF THE VOTING JAR WAS ACCIDENTALLY KNOCKED OVER, THE VOTE WAS REVEALED.

Chicken Rice Salad

2 cups (about) chopped cooked chicken
2 cups chopped celery
2½ cups cooked white rice
½ teaspoon curry powder (optional)
Sliced almonds to taste
Golden raisins to taste
½ cup cooked green peas (optional)
½ cup chutney (optional)
¾ cup Italian salad dressing

Combine the chicken, celery, rice, curry powder, almonds, raisins, peas and chutney in a bowl and mix well.

Add the salad dressing and toss to coat.

Refrigerate, covered, until completely chilled.

Yield: 4 servings

Freddie's Potato Salad

8 to 10 medium red or white potatoes
¼ cup chopped parsley
5 to 6 tablespoons olive oil
2 tablespoons white vinegar
Salt and pepper to taste

Cut the potatoes into 1-inch cubes. Combine with enough water to cover in a saucepan. Bring to a boil. Boil for 15 minutes or until tender; drain.

Combine the warm potatoes, parsley, olive oil, vinegar, salt and pepper in a large bowl and mix well.

Serve warm or at room temperature.

Yield: 4 to 6 servings

Crunchy Apple Salad

1 large unpeeled apple, chopped
1 large rib celery, chopped
1/4 cup peanuts
1/4 cup raisins
1/4 cup mayonnaise
Lettuce leaves
1 cup toasted oat cereal

Combine the apple, celery, peanuts, raisins and mayonnaise in a bowl and mix gently. Chill, covered, until ready to serve.

Arrange lettuce leaves on 4 salad plates. Sprinkle 1/4 cup of the cereal over the lettuce leaves on each plate. Place 1/4 of the apple mixture over the cereal on each plate.

Yield: 4 servings

Rainbow Medley

1 (15-ounce) can unsweetened pineapple chunks, drained
1 (11-ounce) can mandarin oranges, drained
1/2 cup flaked coconut
1/2 cup walnuts or pecans (optional)
3 tablespoons mayonnaise
2 to 3 tablespoons whipped topping
1/2 to 1 cup miniature marshmallows

Combine the pineapple, oranges, coconut and walnuts in a large bowl. Add the mayonnaise and whipped topping and mix gently just until the fruit is coated.

Fold in the marshmallows. Chill, covered, until ready to serve.

Yield: 8 to 10 servings

Beef and Bean Tortilla Roll-Ups

For low-cost eating, choose tortillas! Just use a small amount of meat or poultry mixed with less-expensive ingredients such as beans, salsa and cheese to make a nutritious and delicious filling.

1 onion, chopped
1 garlic clove, chopped
1 tablespoon vegetable oil
5 ounces ground beef
1 (16-ounce) can black beans
1 cup salsa
$1/4$ teaspoon salt
$1/8$ teaspoon pepper
8 small flour tortillas
2 ounces Cheddar cheese, shredded (optional)

Sauté the onion and garlic in the oil in a skillet for 3 minutes. Add the ground beef. Cook until brown, stirring until crumbly; drain. Stir in the undrained beans, $1/2$ cup of the salsa, salt and pepper. Cook over low heat for 10 minutes.

Place the tortillas on a microwave-safe plate. Cover with a damp paper towel. Microwave on High for 45 seconds or until warm, making the tortillas easy to roll.

Spread $1/2$ cup of the ground beef mixture evenly down the center of each tortilla. Sprinkle with the cheese. Roll up the tortillas. Place seam side down on a microsave-safe serving plate. Spoon the remaining $1/2$ cup salsa over the tortillas.

Microwave on High for $1 1/2$ minutes, turning after 45 seconds.

Yield: 4 servings

Bonnie's Beans
and Dogs

1 (8-count) package all-meat hot dogs
1 (30-ounce) can pork and beans
1 (20-ounce) can pineapple chunks

Cut the hot dogs into bite-size pieces.

Combine the hot dogs, pork and beans and pineapple chunks in a slow cooker and stir to combine.

Cook on Low for 2 hours.

Yield: 8 to 10 servings

Pigs in a
Blanket

1 (8-count) can refrigerated dinner rolls
8 all-meat hot dogs
8 (^{1}/4x^1/2x3-inch) strips Cheddar cheese

Separate the dough along the perforations into 8 pieces.

Cut a slit in each hot dog and place a cheese strip in the slit.

Shape 1 piece of dough around each hot dog, pinching the edges to seal. Place on a lightly greased baking sheet.

Bake at 400 degrees for 15 to 20 minutes or until golden brown.

Serve with catsup and mustard.

Yield: 8 servings

Pocket Sandwiches

4 cups cooked ham or turkey strips
4 cups packed torn leaf lettuce
2 medium tomatoes, chopped
2 cups cubed Cheddar cheese
5 (6-inch) pocket bread rounds
Pocket Sandwich Dressing

Combine the ham, lettuce, tomatoes and cheese in a bowl and toss to mix.

Cut the bread rounds into halves. Spoon the ham mixture into the pockets. Drizzle the Pocket Sandwich Dressing over the filling.

Yield: 10 servings

Pocket Sandwich Dressing

$1/4$ cup vegetable oil
2 tablespoons olive oil
2 tablespoons red wine vinegar
2 teaspoons dried salad herbs
$1/2$ teaspoon dry mustard
1 garlic clove, minced
$1/2$ teaspoon salt
$1/4$ teaspoon pepper

Combine the vegetable oil, olive oil, vinegar, salad herbs, dry mustard, garlic, salt and pepper in a bowl and mix well. Store in an airtight container in the refrigerator.

Yield: 10 servings

Bear-Face Pizzas

2 cups tomato sauce
1 teaspoon oregano
½ teaspoon pepper
6 English muffins, split
1 small can black olives, drained
12 slices mozzarella cheese

Combine the tomato sauce, oregano and pepper in a bowl and mix well. Spread on the muffin halves. Slice the olives. Cut a mouth and nose shape from each cheese slice. Arrange the olives and cheese pieces to resemble a face on each muffin half, using the olive slices for eyes. Cut the remaining cheese into small strips and arrange on the muffin halves to look like fur. Place the muffin halves on a baking sheet. Bake at 425 degrees for 5 to 8 minutes or until the sauce is bubbly.

Yield: 12 servings

Egg-in-a-Bun Sandwiches

4 hamburger buns, split
Margarine to taste
4 eggs
Salt and pepper to taste
4 slices cheese

Cut a hole in the top of each bun with a biscuit cutter. Remove the cut portion of the bun top. Spread margarine on the inside bottom half of each bun. Replace the top of the bun.

Place the buns on a baking sheet. Break an egg into each hole. Sprinkle with salt and pepper.

Bake at 325 degrees for 25 minutes. Layer a cheese slice over each cooked egg.

Bake for an additional 5 minutes. Serve hot.

Yield: 4 servings

Peanut Butter Roll-Ups

Peanut butter
4 flour tortillas
Sunflower kernels, dried fruit bits, sliced banana or raisins

Spread peanut butter over 1 side of each tortilla. Sprinkle with sunflower kernels.

Roll each tortilla up to enclose the filling. May cut into bite-size slices.

Yield: 4 servings

DID YOU KNOW...
THAT AMERICANS EAT APPROXIMATELY 12.5 MILLION POUNDS OF CHEESE DAILY? THIS INCLUDES BLEU CHEESE, CREAM CHEESE, SWISS CHEESE, CHEDDAR CHEESE, AND COTTAGE CHEESE.

Banana Split Sandwich

2 to 3 tablespoons peanut butter
1 thick slice whole wheat bread or half a pita
1/2 banana, sliced
Honey or natural fruit syrup to taste
1 tablespoon sunflower kernels
1 tablespoon unsweetened shredded coconut

Spread the peanut butter on the bread slice.

Arrange the banana slices over the peanut butter. Drizzle with honey. Sprinkle the sunflower kernels and coconut over the honey.

Yield: 1 serving

Freddie's Macaroni

8 ounces macaroni
1 cup shredded Cheddar cheese
3/4 cup shredded provolone cheese
1/4 cup grated Romano cheese
1/4 cup (1/2 stick) margarine, cut into pieces
Salt and pepper to taste
1/2 cup crushed potato chips

Cook the macaroni using the package directions; drain. Combine the hot cooked macaroni, Cheddar cheese, provolone cheese, Romano cheese, margarine, salt and pepper in a bowl and mix well. Spoon into an 8x8-inch baking dish sprayed with nonstick cooking spray. Sprinkle with the potato chips. Bake at 350 degrees for 30 minutes.

Yield: 4 servings

Popcorn-Plus Squares

1 cup (2 sticks) butter
1 (16-ounce) package miniature marshmallows
8 cups popped popcorn
1 cup peanuts
1 cup "M&M's" chocolate candies
1 cup gumdrops

Heat the butter and marshmallows in a saucepan over low heat until melted and well blended, stirring constantly.

Combine the popped popcorn, peanuts, candies and gumdrops in a large bowl and toss to mix.

Pour the marshmallow mixture over the popped popcorn mixture and mix well but gently. Press the mixture into a buttered 9x13-inch dish.

Chill in the refrigerator for several hours or until firm. Cut into squares.

Yield: 3 to 4 dozen

Bonnie's Blend

Cheddar goldfish crackers
Bite-size pretzels
Cereal of choice
Peanuts
Gummy bears
Raisins

Combine crackers, pretzels, cereal, peanuts, gummy bears and raisins in a bowl and toss to mix.

Variations: Use different kinds of cereals mixed together, "M&M's" chocolate candies, or different kinds of nuts such as honey-roasted peanuts or cashews.

Yield: Variable

Gelatin Shapes

10 envelopes unflavored gelatin
3 cups cold water
16 ounces apple or cranberry
juice concentrate

Combine the gelatin and cold water in a saucepan. Let stand until the gelatin is softened.

Heat until the gelatin dissolves, stirring constantly.

Pour in the apple juice concentrate and mix well. Pour into a 10x15-inch or other large flat dish.

Chill until firm. Cut into desired shapes with cookie cutters.

Yield: 20 or more shapes

S'More Pudding

Everybody loves s'mores. To make one, you toast a marshmallow over a campfire. Then you put the marshmallow on a graham cracker, cover it with a piece of chocolate and put another graham cracker on top. It's a gooey sandwich of marshmallow and melted chocolate. It tastes so good, you want s'more.

1 cup milk
1 cup milk chocolate chips
15 marshmallows
4 whole graham crackers, crumbled into small pieces

Combine the milk and chocolate chips in a saucepan. Cook over low heat until the chocolate chips are melted, stirring occasionally. Add the marshmallows. Cook until melted and sticky, stirring constantly. Cool to room temperature.

Stir the graham cracker pieces into the pudding. Spoon into serving bowls.

Yield: 4 servings

Creamy Apple Slush

⅓ cup vanilla ice cream, softened
½ cup applesauce
¼ cup milk
¼ teaspoon vanilla extract
Cinnamon to taste
Ginger to taste
Nutmeg to taste

Mash the ice cream with a spoon in a small bowl. Add the applesauce and mix well. Add the milk, vanilla, cinnamon, ginger and nutmeg, stirring until well blended.

Pour into a glass or mug to serve.

Yield: 1 serving

Perky Cinnamon Apple Juice

1 gallon apple juice
1 (1-liter) bottle ginger ale
1 teaspoon whole cloves
2 (3-inch) cinnamon sticks,
broken into pieces
¾ cup red hot cinnamon candies

Combine the apple juice and ginger ale in a 30-cup percolator. Place the cloves, cinnamon and candies in the percolator basket. Perk using manufacturer's directions.

Yield: 25 servings

DID YOU KNOW...
THAT APPROXIMATELY $2.5 BILLION IS SPENT EVERY YEAR BY AMERICAN CHILDREN BETWEEN THE AGES OF FOUR AND TWELVE ON FOOD AND BEVERAGES? ANOTHER $80 BILLION IN PURCHASES IS INFLUENCED BY THIS GROUP.

Candy Cane Cocoa

4 cups milk
3 ounces chocolate, chopped
4 red-and-white-striped peppermint
candies, crushed
Whipped cream
4 small red-and-white-
striped peppermint candy canes

Bring the milk to a simmer in a saucepan. Add the chocolate and crushed peppermint candies. Cook until the mixture is smooth, whisking constantly.

Divide the hot cocoa among 4 mugs. Garnish with whipped cream. Serve with a candy cane to use as a stirring stick.

Yield: 4 servings

Lemonade Special

2 unpeeled lemons, cut into quarters
1½ cups sugar
2 cups milk
Ice
Club soda to taste

Combine the lemons, sugar and milk in a blender container. Process until smooth. Chill, covered, for 1 to 2 days.

Fill each serving glass ¼ full with the lemon mixture. Add ice and club soda and mix well.

Yield: 6 servings

Macaroni Dye

½ cup rubbing alcohol
Large bowl
Food coloring of choice
Uncooked macaroni
Newspaper

Place the alcohol in the large bowl. Add enough food coloring to make of the desired color and stir.

Add the macaroni and mix well. Let stand until macaroni is of the desired color.

Spread on newspaper to dry.

Use for macaroni jewelry or crush for a mosaic picture.

NOT AN EDIBLE RECIPE

Bonnie's Magic Bubbles

2 tablespoons dishwashing detergent
1 cup water
1 teaspoon sugar
1 tablespoon glycerin
Large container
Bubble blowers such as a straw or shaped coat hanger

Combine the detergent, water, sugar and glycerin in a large container. Stir until the sugar dissolves.

Dip the bubble blowers into the soap mixture.

Blow magic bubbles that float well and last a long time.

NOT AN EDIBLE RECIPE

DID YOU KNOW...
THAT MOSAICS ARE BELIEVED TO HAVE ORIGINATED IN THE NEAR EAST AROUND 5,000 YEARS AGO?

Puffy Paint

Flour
Salt
Water
Plastic squeeze bottle
Liquid tempera paint
Heavy paper or cardboard

Combine equal parts of flour, salt and water in the squeeze bottle and mix until smooth.

Add enough paint to make of the desired color and mix well. Place the top on the bottle.

Squeeze into designs on heavy paper or cardboard.

Let stand until dry. The paint will be puffy when dry.

NOT AN EDIBLE RECIPE

Face Paint

6 teaspoons cornstarch
3 teaspoons water
3 teaspoons cold cream
Food colorings of choice
Muffin pan with 6 cups
Paint brushes of different sizes

Combine 1 teaspoon cornstarch, $1/2$ teaspoon water, $1/2$ teaspoon cold cream and 1 to 2 drops of food coloring in each cup of the muffin pan and mix well.

Paint designs on your face using the paint brushes and different colored face paints.

NOT AN EDIBLE RECIPE

DID YOU KNOW...
THAT FACE PAINTING IS NOT NEW? TRIBAL PEOPLES HAVE PAINTED DESIGNS ON THEIR BODIES FOR THOUSANDS OF YEARS. DESIGNS WERE USED FOR DECORATION, FESTIVALS, AND HUNTS.

Handkerchief Parachute

Wooden clothespin
Paintbrush
Tempera paints
Scissors
String
Handkerchief

Paint a "man" on the clothespin using the brush and tempera paints. Let dry.

Cut four 12-inch lengths of string. Tie 1 end of each string to each corner of the handkerchief.

Tie the loose ends of the strings to the top of the clothespin.

Roll up the handkerchief and clothespin. Throw as high as you can. Watch the parachute float down.

NOT AN EDIBLE RECIPE

Fancy Flowerpots

Acrylic paints in gold metallic, dark green and green
Paper plates
Natural sponge
Terra-cotta flowerpots and saucers
Ivy stencil
Stencil brush
Acrylic paint pen in gold

Pour a small amount of gold metallic paint on a paper plate. Dip the sponge lightly in the paint. Apply the paint all over one flowerpot, using a pouncing motion. Repeat the process with the saucer.

Stencil the ivy around the edge of one pot using the dark green and green acrylic paints. Add the tendrils using the gold paint pen.

Repeat the process for the remaining flowerpots and saucers.

NOT AN EDIBLE RECIPE

Lively Lunch Box

Tulip® Paints in Blue Slick, Green Slick,
Pink Slick and Red Slick
4 paper plates
Sponge in a shape of choice
such as a heart or car
Plastic lunch box
Paint brush

Pour a small amount of one paint color on a paper plate. Dip the sponge into the paint and press onto the lunch box. Rinse the sponge. Repeat the process with the remaining paint colors.

Print "LUNCH TIME" on the lunch box in Red Slick paint using the paint brush. Let stand for 24 hours to dry.

NOT AN EDIBLE RECIPE

Freddie's Friends' Apron

Tulip® Slick Paints
Waxed paper or paper plate
Water
Muslin butcher apron
Pencil

Squeeze paint onto waxed paper. Add a few drops of water and mix well. Dip the friend's hand into the paint. Press the hand firmly onto the apron, removing quickly. Repeat the process for each friend.

Draw the friends' names and ages below each handprint lightly with the pencil.

Write "Freddie's Friends" on the apron bib with the pencil.

Outline the pencil marks, squeezing the paint directly from the bottle.

Let dry for 24 hours.

Note: May write "Grandma's Helpers" or other phrase instead of "Freddie's Friends" on the apron bib.

NOT AN EDIBLE RECIPE

Rainbow Wood Greeting Cards

Newspaper
Plain white cards and envelopes
Cardboard
Assorted leaves and ferns
Spray paint

Cover your work surface with newspaper.

Open a card on your work surface.
Cover the back of the card with
a piece of cardboard.

Arrange the leaves and ferns in a
random pattern on the front
of the card. Spray lightly with paint.

Let stand for a few minutes. Remove
the cardboard, leaves and ferns. Repeat
the process with the remaining cards.
Dry the cards thoroughly
before using.

NOT AN EDIBLE RECIPE

Did You Know...
THAT FERNS ARE AN ANCIENT GROUP OF PLANTS
THAT HAVE GROWN ON EARTH FOR MORE
THAN 300 MILLION YEARS?

Slippery Slime

½ cup warm water
½ cup glue
Large bowl
¼ to ½ teaspoon borax
¼ cup warm water
Small bowl
Food coloring of choice

Combine the ½ cup warm water and glue in a large bowl and mix well.

Combine the borax and ¼ cup warm water in a small bowl, stirring until the borax dissolves completely.

Add the borax mixture and a drop of food coloring to the glue mixture and mix well.

May add additional borax to the mixture to make the slime thicker.

NOT AN EDIBLE RECIPE

Gooey Goop

Cornstarch
Water
Food coloring (optional)
Bowl

Combine enough cornstarch, water and food coloring in a bowl to make of the desired consistency and color.

Work the dough to create different forms and designs. This dough has characteristics of both a solid and a liquid.

NOT AN EDIBLE RECIPE

Pinecone Ornament

Newspaper
1 pinecone
Gold spray paint
2⅓ yards (⅛-inch-wide) red
satin ribbon
Hot-glue gun
1 small cluster of white silk flowers
with leaves
2 small white silk rosebuds
Dried baby's breath

Cover your work surface with the newspaper.

Place the pinecone on the newspaper. Spray with the gold spray paint, covering completely.

Form a small multi-looped bow with the red satin ribbon, leaving 6-inch tails. Glue the bow to the top of the pinecone.

Glue the cluster of silk flowers to the top of the pinecone. Glue the rosebuds to the cluster of flowers. Glue the baby's breath among the flowers.

NOT AN EDIBLE RECIPE

Cinnamon Alligator Ornaments

1 cup ground cinnamon
2 tablespoons ground allspice
Bowl
1 cup applesauce
¼ cup craft glue
Rolling pin and waxed paper
Alligator cookie cutter
Drinking straw
Whole cloves

Combine the cinnamon and allspice in a bowl and mix well. Add the apple-sauce and glue and mix well, adding additional water and glue if needed to make of a clay-like consistency.

Roll out dough between sheets of waxed paper to ½-inch thickness. Remove top sheet of waxed paper. Cut with alligator cookie cutter. Remove excess dough. Make holes with the straw for hanging. Insert cloves for eyes. Air dry on a flat surface for a few days or until completely dry.

NOT AN EDIBLE RECIPE

LET'S TALK ABOUT THE DAY

Pete and Patsy Possum

Dinner & Crafts

Extra-Easy Lasagna

12 ounces ground beef
3 cups spaghetti sauce
6 lasagna noodles
15 ounces ricotta cheese
2 cups shredded mozzarella cheese
1/4 cup water

Brown the ground beef in a skillet over medium-high heat, stirring until crumbly; drain. Add the spaghetti sauce. Cook until heated through, stirring occasionally.

Spread 1 1/2 cups of the ground beef mixture into a rectangular 2-quart baking dish. Top with 3 noodles, half the ricotta cheese and half the mozzarella cheese. Repeat the layers.

Top with the remaining meat sauce. Pour the water around the edges gradually. Bake, covered with foil, at 375 degrees for 45 minutes; remove the cover. Bake for 10 minutes longer.

Let stand for 10 minutes before serving.

Yield: 8 servings

DID YOU KNOW...
THAT PASTA COMES IN MORE THAN 600 SHAPES AND CAN BE BAKED, BOILED, STEAMED, STUFFED, SMOTHERED WITH SAUCE, FRIED, SPICED, OR EVEN DIPPED IN CHOCOLATE? IT CAN BE USED FOR ANY COURSE FROM APPETIZER THROUGH MAIN DISH TO SALADS AND DESSERTS.

Hamburger Surprise

1½ pounds ground beef
1 egg
½ cup seasoned bread crumbs
¼ teaspoon salt
¼ teaspoon pepper
4 ounces mozzarella cheese,
cut into cubes

Combine the ground beef, egg,
bread crumbs, salt and pepper
in a bowl and mix well.

Divide into 12 equal portions. Shape
each portion into a 3-inch patty.
Top each of 6 patties with an equal
amount of the cheese cubes. Place the
remaining patties over the cheese,
pressing the edges to seal.

Grill over hot coals until done to taste,
turning once. May be baked in a
350-degree oven for 30 minutes.

Yield: 6 servings

DID YOU KNOW...
THAT ELVIS PRESLEY'S FAVORITE FOOD
WAS A COMPLETELY CHARRED HAMBURGER?

Shepherd's Pie

8 ounces ground beef
5 or 6 large red potatoes, peeled
Salt to taste
1/2 cup rice milk
2 to 3 tablespoons milk-free margarine such as Promise Ultra Fat-Free Margarine
1 (8- to 10-ounce) can sweet yellow corn
1 teaspoon salt

Brown the ground beef in a skillet, stirring until crumbly; drain.

Combine the potatoes with enough water to cover in a saucepan. Bring to a boil. Boil until tender; drain. Combine the potatoes, salt to taste, rice milk and margarine in a mixer bowl and beat until smooth.

Combine the corn and cooked ground beef in an 8x8-inch baking dish. Sprinkle with the 1 teaspoon salt. Spread the mashed potatoes over the top.

Bake at 350 degrees for 10 minutes for a crusty topping.

Yield: 3 to 4 servings

Oven-Fried Sesame Chicken

2 tablespoons flour
3 tablespoons sesame seeds
1/4 teaspoon pepper
4 chicken breasts, skinned
2 tablespoons soy sauce
2 tablespoons (1/4 stick) melted reduced-calorie margarine

Combine the flour, sesame seeds and pepper in a bowl and mix well.

Dip the chicken breasts in the soy sauce in a shallow bowl. Coat well with the sesame seed mixture.

Arrange bone side down in a shallow 9x9-inch baking dish. Drizzle with the margarine.

Bake at 400 degrees for 40 to 45 minutes or until cooked through.

Yield: 4 servings

Chicken, Spaghetti and Green Stuff

8 ounces thin spaghetti
1/2 cup (1 stick) butter or margarine
2 cups chopped cooked chicken
1 (4-ounce) can sliced mushrooms
1/4 cup chopped fresh parsley
1 garlic clove, minced
1/4 cup dry white wine (optional)
1/2 cup grated Parmesan cheese
2/3 cup milk
Dash of pepper

Cook the spaghetti using the package directions; drain. Melt 2 tablespoons of the butter in a large skillet. Add the chicken, undrained mushrooms, parsley and garlic. Cook until the chicken is lightly browned, stirring frequently. Add the wine. Cook for 3 minutes, stirring constantly. Spoon into a bowl.

Melt the remaining 6 tablespoons butter in a skillet. Add the cheese, milk and pepper. Cook over low heat until the cheese is melted and the sauce is smooth, stirring constantly. Pour over the chicken mixture and mix well. Add the hot cooked spaghetti to the chicken mixture. Toss gently to mix.

Yield: 4 to 6 servings

Chicken Nuggets

Vegetable oil for deep-frying
$\frac{1}{3}$ cup water
1 egg
$\frac{1}{3}$ cup flour
2 teaspoons sesame seeds
$1\frac{1}{2}$ teaspoons paprika
$1\frac{1}{2}$ teaspoons salt
2 chicken breast fillets

Preheat the oil to 375 degrees in a deep fryer. Whisk the water and egg in a small bowl. Mix the flour, sesame seeds, paprika and salt in a bowl. Cut the chicken into 1x1$\frac{1}{2}$-inch pieces. Dip each chicken nugget into the egg mixture. Coat well with the flour mixture.

Drop 5 or 6 nuggets at a time into the hot oil. Deep-fry for 4 minutes or until golden brown; drain on paper towels. Serve hot or cold.

Yield: 3 servings

DID YOU KNOW...
THAT FOR AT LEAST FOUR THOUSAND YEARS CHICKENS HAVE BEEN RAISED DOMESTICALLY?

Chicken Potpie

⅓ cup milk-free margarine such as Promise Ultra Fat-Free Margarine
⅓ cup chopped onion
⅓ cup flour
½ teaspoon salt
1¾ cups chicken broth
⅔ cup rice milk
2 to 3 cups chopped cooked chicken
1 (10-ounce) package frozen peas and carrots
2 (9-inch) all ready pie pastries

Heat the margarine in a skillet until melted. Sauté the onion in the margarine for 1 to 2 minutes or until translucent.

Add the flour and salt. Cook until bubbly, stirring constantly. Reduce the heat.

Whisk in the broth and rice milk. Cook over low heat until thickened, whisking constantly. Remove from the heat. Add the chicken and peas and carrots and mix well.

Fit one of the pie pastries into a 9x9-inch baking pan. Spoon the chicken mixture into the pie pastry. Top with the remaining pastry, sealing the edges and cutting vents.

Bake at 425 degrees for 35 minutes or until golden brown. Let stand for 10 to 15 minutes.

Yield: 6 servings

Did You Know...
THAT IN 1929 CLARENCE BIRDSEYE PERFECTED THE PROCESS OF FREEZING VEGETABLES?

Turkey Casserole

2 cups Really Easy Bread Stuffing
8 slices cooked turkey
2 cups turkey gravy
1 (8-ounce) can cranberry sauce, sliced
Salt and pepper to taste
4 cups mashed cooked potatoes

Spread the stuffing in an 8x8-inch baking dish. Layer the turkey and gravy over the stuffing.

Arrange the cranberry sauce over the gravy. Sprinkle with salt and pepper. Top with the mashed potatoes.

Bake at 350 degrees for 30 to 40 minutes or until the potatoes are golden brown and the casserole is heated through.

Yield: 8 servings

Really Easy Bread Stuffing

1 (16-ounce) loaf white bread
1 onion, finely chopped
1 teaspoon poultry seasoning
Pinch of salt
Pinch of pepper

Tear the bread into small pieces. Combine the torn bread with enough water to completely moisten in a bowl. Add the onion, poultry seasoning, salt and pepper and mix well.

Place the stuffing on a large piece of foil. Fold over the edges and seal to enclose the stuffing. Bake at 325 degrees for 1 hour. May open the foil after 45 minutes to brown and crisp the top.

May place the unbaked stuffing in a turkey if desired.

Yield: 6 to 8 servings

Spaghetti

1 pound ground turkey
2 (26-ounce) cans spaghetti sauce
1 teaspoon cinnamon
2 teaspoons brown sugar
16 ounces spaghetti, hot, cooked

Brown the ground turkey in a large skillet, stirring until crumbly.

Add the spaghetti sauce, cinnamon and brown sugar and mix well. Simmer for several minutes.

Serve over hot cooked spaghetti.

Yield: 4 to 6 servings

Tuna and Macaroni Casserole

1 (7-ounce) package macaroni and cheese dinner
¼ cup (½ stick) butter
¼ cup milk
1 (6-ounce) can water-pack tuna, drained, flaked
1 (3-ounce) can grated American cheese
Onion salt and pepper to taste

Prepare the macaroni and cheese dinner with the butter and milk using the package directions. Add the tuna and mix well. Pour into a greased 2-quart baking dish.

Sprinkle with the cheese, onion salt and pepper. Bake at 325 degrees for 20 minutes or until bubbly.

Yield: 6 servings

Fried Fish

1 egg
¹⁄₃ cup mustard
¹⁄₂ teaspoon seasoned salt
4 fish fillets
1 cup instant potato flakes
Vegetable oil for frying

Combine the egg, mustard and seasoned salt in a bowl and mix well.

Dip the fish in the egg mixture. Coat well with the potato flakes.

Fry in the hot oil in a skillet until golden brown on both sides. Drain on paper towels.

Yield: 4 servings

Shrimp Boats

This dish is perfect for children with allergies.

1 medium avocado
1 teaspoon lemon juice
Salt and pepper to taste
1 (4-ounce) can tiny shrimp, drained
Cocktail sauce

Cut the avocado into halves and remove the pit. Sprinkle with lemon juice, salt and pepper. Combine the shrimp with enough cocktail sauce to coat in a bowl.

Spoon the shrimp mixture into the center of the halves where the pit was. May top with additional lemon juice and cocktail sauce.

Yield: 1 serving

DID YOU KNOW...
THAT THERE ARE MORE THAN **600** SPECIES OF EDIBLE FISH IN THE WATERS AROUND THE UNITED STATES AND **3,000** WORLDWIDE?

Possum Pasta

This will keep for up to 2 days. Reheat in a steamer or double boiler.

3 tablespoons olive oil
2 garlic cloves, minced (optional)
3 cups sliced zucchini
2 cups broccoli florets
1 cup (¹/₂-inch-long) asparagus pieces
2¹/₂ cups chopped yellow squash
1 cup small green peas
8 ounces linguini or spaghetti
2¹/₂ cups chopped tomatoes
2 tablespoons chopped fresh basil, or
1 tablespoon dried
Olive oil (optional)
Feta cheese (optional)
Grated Parmesan cheese (optional)
Oil and vinegar dressing (optional)
Freshly ground pepper (optional)
Minced garlic (optional)

Heat 2 tablespoons of the olive oil in a large skillet or saucepan. Sauté 2 cloves garlic in the hot oil. Add the zucchini, broccoli, asparagus, squash and peas. Sauté for 8 minutes or until the vegetables are tender-crisp.

Fill a large pot with enough water to cook the pasta. Bring to a boil. Add the remaining 1 tablespoon olive oil. Break the linguini into halves. Add to the pot. Cook until al dente; drain.

Combine the hot cooked pasta with the sautéed vegetables in a large bowl. Add the tomatoes and basil and mix well. Add additional olive oil, feta cheese, Parmesan cheese, oil and vinegar dressing, pepper and additional garlic and mix well. Serve hot.

Yield: 6 servings

Spastic Elastic

½ cup Elmer's glue
½ cup (or less) liquid starch
Food coloring of choice
Bowl
Spoon

Combine the glue, starch and food coloring in a bowl.

Stir with a spoon until the mixture begins to thicken. Lift from bowl.

Knead and stretch until thickened to the desired consistency.

Mold and shape as desired.

Store in airtight containers such as plastic eggs.

NOT AN EDIBLE RECIPE

Pete and Patsy's Play Food

1 cup dry milk powder
1 cup peanut butter
½ cup honey
Bowl

Combine the dry milk powder, peanut butter and honey in a bowl.

Mix with your hands until smooth.

May be eaten if played with on a clean surface and with clean hands.

Play Dough

1 cup flour
¼ cup salt
2 tablespoons cream of tartar
Saucepan
Spoon
1 cup water
2 teaspoons food coloring of choice
1 tablespoon vegetable oil
Flour

Combine 1 cup flour, salt and cream of tartar in a saucepan and mix well with a spoon.

Add the water, food coloring and oil and mix well.

Cook over medium heat for 3 to 5 minutes or until the mixture forms a ball, stirring constantly.

Remove from the heat. Place the play dough on a floured surface and knead until smooth.

Store in an airtight container in the refrigerator.

Variations:

Sparkle Play Dough—Add glitter with the flour.

Scented Play Dough—Add a flavored drink mix with the flour.

Button Frame

Newspaper
Crafter's cement
Assorted buttons
1 (5x7-inch) clear acrylic frame

Cover your work surface with newspaper.

Cement the buttons randomly around the edge of the frame, overlapping as desired. Buttons may be moved slightly before the cement sets.

Allow the cement to dry thoroughly.

NOT AN EDIBLE RECIPE

Buttons and Buttons Barrette

Newspaper
Hot glue gun
Buttons of various sizes and shapes
1 (3-inch) spring-clasp hair barrette

Cover your work surface with newspaper.

Glue the buttons randomly to the barrette, creating multiple layers and overlapping as desired.

Allow the glue to dry thoroughly.

NOT AN EDIBLE RECIPE

DID YOU KNOW...
THE BIGGEST BUBBLE-GUM BUBBLE EVERY BLOWN
WAS TWENTY-TWO INCHES AROUND?

Ribboned
Banana Clip

Scissors
6 yards (³⁄₈-inch-wide) green
satin ribbon
6 yards (³⁄₈-inch-wide) red satin ribbon
6 yards (³⁄₈-inch-wide) white
satin ribbon
1 (7-inch-long) banana hair clip

Cut each ribbon into 9-inch lengths.

Wrap one 9-inch length between each tooth of the banana clip and knot in the middle, leaving ends of equal length. Repeat the process until all the ribbon has been used, alternating ribbon colors.

NOT AN EDIBLE RECIPE

Treasure
Box

Sturdy box of desired size
Self-adhesive paper
Scissors
Stickers of choice

Cover the box with the adhesive paper, cutting to fit.

Arrange the stickers over the adhesive paper as desired.

Place your treasures from the day in the box.

NOT AN EDIBLE RECIPE

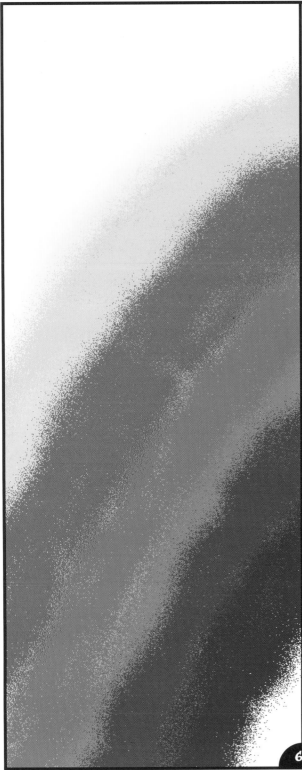

Leather-Look
Pencil Holder

Metal fruit or vegetable can
Pliers
Wide masking tape
Brown shoe polish and cloth rag

Bend back and smooth any raw cut edge on the can with pliers. Clean and dry the can thoroughly.

Tear the masking tape into irregular pieces and apply them randomly over the entire can, inside and out. Overlap the tape pieces and add as many layers as needed to get the desired effect.

Apply a heavy coat of shoe polish to the holder with the rag to give the appearance of leather. Wipe off any excess polish and let dry. Use the holder for storing pencils.

NOT AN EDIBLE RECIPE

DID YOU KNOW...
THAT THE LEAD IN PENCILS WE USE TODAY IS REALLY A MIXTURE OF GRAPHITE, CLAY, AND WAX—WHICH ISN'T LEAD AT ALL?

Patsy's Pillar Candles

Gemstones with nailhead settings
Metallic nailheads
Pillar candles in desired colors and sizes
Rubber band and small ruler

Determine the style of the desired arrangement of the nailheads.

For free-form arrangements, position nailheads on each candle and press firmly in place. For geometric arrangements, indicate positions by placing a rubber band around the top of each candle and marking vertical measurements on the band.

Mark horizontal positions on the ruler. Place the ruler along each candle at marks on the rubber band to align nailheads and use the ruler as a guide, pressing the nailheads firmly into the candle.

NOT AN EDIBLE RECIPE

DID YOU KNOW...
THAT IT IS BELIEVED THAT CANDLES WERE FIRST USED BY THE EGYPTIANS AROUND 3000 B.C.?

Ribbon Bookmark

14 inches (³/₈-inch-wide) satin ribbon
Hot-glue gun or white craft glue
Pre-cut and pre-painted wooden craft decoration
Scissors

Fold the ribbon in half to make a 7-inch bookmark. Glue the ribbon together.

Glue the wooden craft decoration at the folded edge.

Trim the ends of the ribbon in a V shape.

NOT AN EDIBLE RECIPE

Wooden Bookmark

Newspaper
Wood stain
6-inch wooden craft stick
Pre-cut and pre-painted wooden craft decoration
Black marker

Cover your work surface with newspaper.

Stain the craft stick. Let dry.

Glue the wooden craft decoration to one end.

Print a name or message with the black marker.

NOT AN EDIBLE RECIPE

DID YOU KNOW...
THAT AMERICA'S FIRST BOOK CLUB WAS FOUNDED IN APRIL 1926 AND WAS THE BOOK-OF-THE-MONTH CLUB?

I'LL SEE YOU IN MY DREAMS

Lounging Louie

Desserts & Bedtime Snacks

Bedtime at Rainbow Wood

By Michael W. Surette

Chef Freddie had been busy all day. The Rainbow Wood picnic was tomorrow and he had been cooking all sorts of goodies and treats. He was expecting a few of his little friends for a sleepover so they could go to the picnic together.

So there Freddie was putting the last bit of frosting on one of his famous Gator cakes when he heard this noise coming down the path. "Flip flop quack, flip flop quack, flip flop quack, flip flop quack."

"That must be one of my guests," Freddie said to himself. He put down his frosting tube, wiped his hands on his apron and hurried to the door. Opening it without waiting for a knock, Freddie stepped outside to greet his guest. Coming up the walkway was Louie the Duck. "A good afternoon to you," exclaimed Freddie. "The same to you," said Louie. "I hope I'm not too early." "Early Shmurlee," said Freddie. "My door is always open as well as my kitchen. Now please, come in. I have your favorite chair all ready and the cookies are still warm."

As Freddie led Louie into the parlor, he heard another noise coming down the path. "Blub-a-dub dubble, dub-a-bub bubble, blub-a-dub dubble, dub-a-bub bubble."

Freddie went back out to see what this noise was all about. Walking up the path by the gate was Bonnie the Bear, blowing bubbles as she went.

"Ah Bonnie Bubbles, so nice to see you," said Freddie. "Please come in." "Thank you berry much, Freddie," replied Bonnie. "Do

you mind if I bring my bottle-o-bubbles in? I promise to keep the cap on tight." "Not a problem at all," said Freddie. "My door is always open as well as my kitchen, even for a bottle-o-bubbles."

So Freddie and Bonnie went into the house. Freddie went into the kitchen to fetch some cookies while Bonnie sat down with Louie. As he was putting the plate of cookies down, Freddie heard another noise coming down the path. "Whizzz wheee meooow, whizzz wheee meooow, whizzz wheee meooow."

Freddie ran out to see what all the racket was. Coming through the gate like a rocket was none other than Ally the Cat. The best skateboarding cat this side of Rainbow Wood. Ally cruised right up the walkway, tipped the front of her skateboard down, and stopped right in front of Freddie.

"Good to see you, Ally," said Freddie. "You do impress me on that skateboard of yours."

"Why thank you, Frederick," said Ally. "You say you're impressed by my skateboarding and I say to that, if I can skateboard half as good as you can cook, my friend, then I guess I'm doing better than better."

"Why thank you, Ally," said Freddie. "Speaking of cooking, I have some nice warm cookies with milk on the way. You can join Louie and Bonnie in the parlor."

"Would it be a problem if I put my skateboard just inside the front door?" asked Ally. "No problem at all," answered Freddie. "I've always said, my door is always open as well as my kitchen even for a skateboard."

So everyone gathered in the parlor and enjoyed Freddie's warm cookies and cold milk. As Freddie was coming out with a third plate of cookies, he heard another noise coming down the path. "Pitter patter pitter patter crunch, pitter patter pitter patter crunch, pitter patter pitter patter crunch."

Freddie left the cookies with his friends and went out to see what the noise was. There coming down the path, arm in arm, tails all-a-twirled, taking turns munching on a pear, were Pete and Patsy Possum.

"Pete and Patsy, so nice to see you," said Freddie. "It's nice to see you," said Pete. "Always a pleasure," said Patsy. "I hope we didn't keep you waiting. We lost track of time searching for the juiciest pear on our favorite tree. We wanted one to share on the walk over." "There's nothing like a pear to share," added Pete.

"Well, you didn't keep me waiting, as everyone has just recently arrived," said Freddie. "And as far as your pear, it looks like a real beauty, what's left of it. I do admire how you two share all the time."

"Well," Pete said, "our mother always tells us—To care is to share and to share is to care. And besides, sharing is fun."

"Speaking of sharing," said Freddie, "I have some nice warm cookies and cold milk already out and I also have a nice big oak branch set up in the corner for your comfort. As I've always said, my door is always open as well as my kitchen."

So there everyone was, in Chef Freddie's parlor, talking about the upcoming picnic. "I hope they have the three-legged race again," said Pete and Patsy. "How about the treasure hunt," added Louie. "There's nothing like looking in the sand for a shiny new nickel." "Yeah, all that stuff is great," said Ally, "but I like the music and the ice cream cones the best."

"You said it," said Bonnie Bubbles. "I love the ice cream, macaroni, potato salad, the pies; oh, everything that Freddie cooks up is just great! But the best of the best, the tastiest of the tastiest, the most magical of all is the Gator cakes with his famous rainbow frosting. Yummy yummy!" Everyone had to agree with that. The Gator cakes were super delicious.

"Frederick my good man," said Ally. "How do you make them taste so good? What's the secret?"

Well, Freddie just kind of sat back in his chair, put his chin in his hand, and looked at all his friends with that sparkle in his eye. "Well, you know," Freddie began, "every chef has dozens of dishes that he doesn't mind making. Then there's a few that he really likes to make. But there's always one that a chef just loves to make. From the bottom of my toes all the way to the tip of my chef's hat, I just love to make Gator cakes and I think that is what makes them so special."

"Well, what do you put in them that tastes so sweet?" asked Bonnie. "And how do you get them to be so chewy?" added Louie.

"So I see," answered Freddie, "you actually want to know what I put in my Gator cakes. Well, the recipe has been in my family for many many years. It actually goes back to my great-great-grandmother Frederica and has been passed all the way down to me. The only problem is that the ingredients have been kept secret for all those years. But since you're all such good friends, I will tell you the most important ingredient of all . . . love. When I make them, I use a little bit of this, a little bit of that, and a whole lot of love."

"Well, it sure shows," said Pete. "You can say that again," added Patsy. "Well, it sure shows," said Pete. Everyone laughed and went on talking about the picnic and everything else that was going on in the Rainbow Wood.

As is always the way when friends gather, the time went by very fast. Before anyone had realized, the moon was very high in the sky and Bonnie Bubbles started a yawn that went around the room quite a few times.

Freddie stood up and said, "Friends, we could go on talking until my whole batch of cookies is gone but I think we would all be better off if we get some sleep. The picnic starts mid-morning and I have carts and carts of food to get to the picnic area."

So Freddie went into the back room to get his friends some pillows and blankets. Pete and Patsy climbed up on the oak branch and hung upside down as possums do. Louie lounged back in his favorite cushy chair with a content smile. Ally lay down at one end of the sofa while Bonnie Bubbles cuddled at the other end.

Freddie came back and went around the room giving out pillows and blankets. He said "good night and sleep tight" to all his friends and turned down the lamp on the mantel.

"Freddie?" Bonnie asked. "Are you going to sleep now, too?"

"Bonnie my dear," Freddie answered. "I just have to ready a few things in the kitchen for the morning and I'll be going, too. And one thing is for sure, when I close my eyes and fall asleep, I'll see you all in my dreams."

THE END…for now

ABOUT THE AUTHOR

MICHAEL W. SURETTE LIVES IN NASHUA, NEW HAMPSHIRE, WITH HIS WIFE MELISSA AND HIS THREE CHILDREN, MICHAEL, CHRISTIN, AND JOSHUA.

I WAS OFFERED THE OPPORTUNITY TO WRITE A SHORT STORY ABOUT CHEF FREDDIE AND HIS FRIENDS UNDER THE RAINBOW.

IN WRITING THIS STORY, MY INTENTION WAS NOT ONLY TO GIVE EACH OF THESE CHARACTERS THEIR OWN PERSONALITY BUT TO ALSO SHOW THE IMPORTANCE OF SHARING, HOSPITALITY, FRIENDSHIP, AND LOVE.

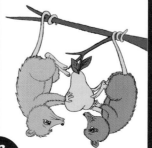

Cake Diagram

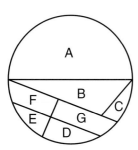

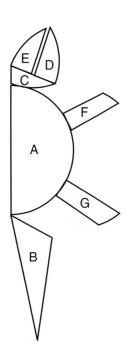

Gator Cake

3 cups flour
1 tablespoon baking powder
½ teaspoon salt
4 eggs
1 cup shortening
2 cups sugar
2 teaspoons vanilla extract
1 cup milk
Gator Icing
Gumdrops, sugar cubes, licorice and assorted candies for decorating

Line the outside of a 9-inch springform pan with foil. Grease and flour the inside of the pan.

Combine the flour, baking powder and salt in a bowl and mix well.

Beat the eggs in a 1-cup measure to lubricate the cup for shortening. Pour the eggs into a large mixer bowl. Fill the 1-cup measure with shortening and add to the eggs. Stir in the sugar. Beat until creamy.

Add the flour mixture and mix well. Stir in the vanilla and milk. Beat at medium speed for 5 minutes or longer, scraping the bowl occasionally (the longer the beating time, the lighter and higher the cake).

Spoon the batter into the prepared pan. Bake at 350 degrees for 45 minutes or until a wooden pick inserted in the center comes out clean. Cool in the pan for 10 minutes. Remove the cake from the pan. Freeze the cake for 45 minutes before cutting to prevent crumbling.

Cut the cake as indicated on the diagram. Stick the parts together using Gator Icing. Frost the top and sides of the gator. Decorate with gumdrops, sugar cubes, licorice and assorted candies using a gumdrop for the eye and licorice for the teeth and claws. Sprinkle with lots of love.

Yield: 8 servings

Gator Icing

¹/₂ cup (1 stick) butter, softened
¹/₂ cup shortening
4 cups confectioners' sugar
1 teaspoon vanilla extract
2 tablespoons milk
Green food coloring

Beat the butter and shortening in a mixer bowl.

Add the confectioners' sugar ¹/₂ at a time, mixing well after each addition.

Add the vanilla and milk and mix well. Add enough food coloring to make of the desired shade of green.

Note: You can make your own rainbow icing like Chef Freddie by dividing the icing, before the green food coloring is added, into several portions and tinting each portion a different color.

Dirt Cake

This project is fun for a group of kids!

1 small or medium plastic window box
1 or 2 (9x13-inch) chocolate cakes
16 ounces nondairy whipped topping
4 cups prepared chocolate pudding
1 (21-ounce) package Oreo cookies,
finely crushed
Gummy worms
An assortment of silk flowers
1 hand-held garden shovel or hoe

Line the bottom of the window box with plastic wrap.

Layer the cake, nondairy whipped topping, pudding and crushed cookies $\frac{1}{2}$ at a time in the window box, completely covering the top with the crushed cookies to look like dirt.

Arrange the gummy worms over the crushed cookies. Arrange the flowers on top.

Serve with the garden shovel.

Yield: Variable

Gumdrop Cake

2 cups (4 sticks) butter
2 cups sugar
4 eggs
2 teaspoons vanilla extract
8 cups flour
1/2 teaspoon ground cloves
1/2 teaspoon nutmeg
1 teaspoon salt
2 teaspoons cinnamon
2 tablespoons baking soda
2 tablespoons hot water
3 cups applesauce
2 pounds gumdrops with black and
white gumdrops discarded
2 pounds raisins
2 cups chopped pecans

Cream the butter and sugar in a mixer bowl. Add the eggs and vanilla and beat until smooth.

Combine the flour, cloves, nutmeg, salt and cinnamon in a bowl and mix well. Add to the creamed mixture gradually and beat until smooth.

Dissolve the baking soda in the hot water in a bowl. Add the baking soda mixture and applesauce to the batter.

Fold the gumdrops, raisins and pecans into the batter.

Divide the batter evenly among 4 greased and floured loaf pans.

Bake at 300 degrees for 3 hours. Let cool on a wire rack.

Yield: 48 servings

Apple Pie

7 or 8 medium apples,
such as McIntosh
²/₃ cup sugar
¹/₃ cup flour
¹/₂ teaspoon nutmeg
¹/₂ teaspoon cinnamon
Dash of salt
2 (9-inch) all ready pie pastries
2 tablespoons (about) butter flavor
vegetable shortening

Cut the apples into thin slices.

Combine the sugar, flour, nutmeg, cinnamon and salt in a bowl and mix well. Add the apples and toss to coat.

Fit 1 pie pastry into a 9-inch pie plate. Spoon the apple mixture into the pastry-lined pie plate. Dot with the shortening. Top with the remaining pastry, sealing the edge and cutting vents. Cover the edge with foil to prevent burning.

Bake at 425 degrees for 40 minutes. Remove the foil. Bake for 10 minutes longer or until golden brown and bubbly.

Yield: 6 servings

DID YOU KNOW...
THAT THE FIRST AMERICAN APPLE ORCHARD WAS PLANTED IN THE EARLY 1600s ON BEACON HILL, WHICH OVERLOOKS BOSTON HARBOR?

Peanut Butter Pie

8 ounces cream cheese, softened
½ cup creamy peanut butter
½ cup confectioners' sugar
16 ounces nondairy whipped topping
1 (8- or 9-inch) graham cracker crust
Miniature peanut butter cups

Combine the cream cheese, peanut butter and confectioners' sugar in a bowl and mix until smooth. Fold in half the whipped topping.

Spoon the peanut butter mixture into the piecrust. Spread the remaining whipped topping over the peanut butter mixture. Top with the peanut butter cups.

Chill, covered, for 2 to 10 hours.

Yield: 6 servings

DID YOU KNOW...
THAT THE WORD GOOBER, A SYNONYM FOR PEANUT, IS DERIVED FROM THE AFRICAN WORD NGUBA? IT IS ONE OF THE FEW AFRICAN WORDS STILL RETAINED IN ENGLISH.

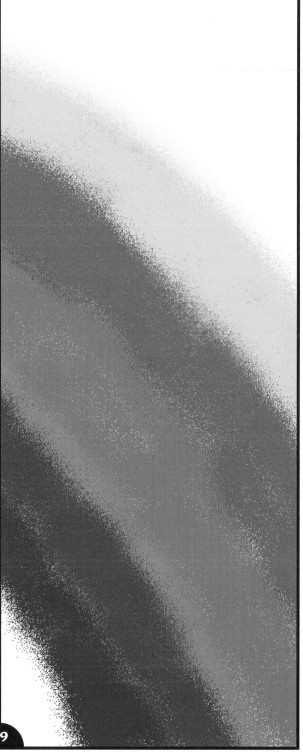

Easy Apple Crisp

1 teaspoon cinnamon
$\frac{1}{2}$ cup sugar
1 cup warm water
8 apples, sliced
$\frac{1}{2}$ cup sugar
$\frac{3}{4}$ cup flour
5 tablespoons butter

Combine the cinnamon, $\frac{1}{2}$ cup sugar and warm water in a bowl and mix well. Add the apples and stir to coat. Pour into an 8x8-inch baking dish.

Combine the $\frac{1}{2}$ cup sugar and flour in a bowl and mix well. Cut in the butter with a fork until crumbly. Sprinkle over the apple mixture.

Bake at 350 degrees for 50 minutes.

Yield: 6 servings

Acorn Magic Delights

1 cup (2 sticks) butter or margarine
$\frac{3}{4}$ cup packed brown sugar
$1\frac{1}{2}$ cups pecans, finely chopped
1 teaspoon vanilla extract
$2\frac{1}{2}$ cups flour
$\frac{1}{2}$ teaspoon baking powder
1 cup semisweet chocolate chips

Melt the butter in a saucepan over low heat. Beat the melted butter, brown sugar, $\frac{3}{4}$ cup of the pecans and vanilla in a mixer bowl until blended. Beat in the flour and baking powder.

Shape the dough into 1-inch balls. Press the balls onto nonstick cookie sheets, flattening slightly and pinching the tops to resemble acorns. Bake at 375 degrees for 10 to 12 minutes. Cool on a wire rack.

Heat the chocolate chips in a double boiler over hot water, stirring until smooth. Remove from the heat. Dip the large ends of the cooled cookies into the melted chocolate. Roll in the remaining $\frac{3}{4}$ cups pecans to coat. Cool to set the chocolate.

Yield: 3 dozen

Baby Ruth Cookies

1⅓ cups flour
½ teaspoon salt
½ teaspoon baking soda
½ cup (1 stick) butter or margarine
¾ cup sugar
1 egg
½ teaspoon vanilla extract
2 bite-size Baby Ruth
candy bars, chopped

Combine the flour, salt and baking soda in a bowl and mix well.

Cream the butter and sugar in a mixer bowl until light and fluffy. Beat in the egg and vanilla. Add the flour mixture and mix well. Stir in the candy.

Drop by heaping teaspoonfuls onto nonstick cookie sheets. Bake at 375 degrees for 12 to 15 minutes.

Yield: 2 dozen

DID YOU KNOW...
THAT THE BABY RUTH CANDY BAR WAS NAMED FOR PRESIDENT GROVER CLEVELAND'S DAUGHTER, WHO WAS BORN IN THE WHITE HOUSE?

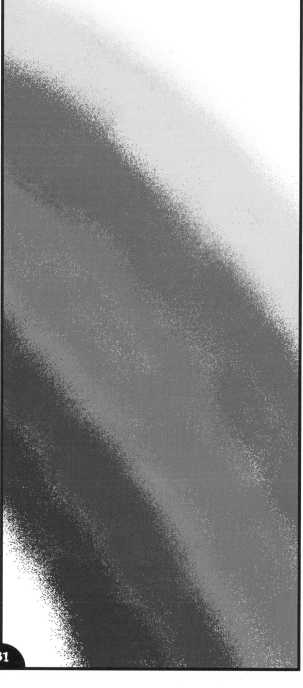

Candy Cane Cookies

1/2 cup (1 stick) butter or margarine,
softened
1/2 cup shortening
1 cup confectioners' sugar
1 egg
1 1/2 teaspoons almond extract
1 teaspoon vanilla extract
2 1/2 cups flour
1 teaspoon salt
1/2 teaspoon red food coloring
1/2 cup crushed peppermint candy
1/2 cup sugar

Combine the butter, shortening, sugar, egg, almond extract and vanilla in a bowl and mix well. Add the flour and salt and mix well.

Divide the dough into 2 equal portions. Combine 1 portion with the red food coloring in a bowl and mix well.

Roll 1 teaspoon of dough from each color into a 4-inch rope on a lightly floured surface. Press the ropes together gently and twist. Place on a nonstick cookie sheet, curving the top to form a candy cane. Repeat the process with the remaining dough.

Bake at 375 degrees for 9 minutes or until light brown. Combine the candy and sugar in a bowl and mix well. Sprinkle over the warm cookies. Cool on a wire rack.

Yield: 4 dozen

Chocolate Chip Cookies

1½ teaspoons Ener-G Egg Replacer
2 tablespoons water
1¾ cups flour
1 teaspoon salt
¾ teaspoon baking soda
¾ cup butter-flavor shortening
1¼ cups packed light brown sugar
2 tablespoons rice milk
1 tablespoon vanilla extract
1 cup carob chocolate chips

Combine the Ener-G Egg Replacer and the water in a bowl and mix well.

Combine the flour, salt and baking soda in a bowl and mix well.

Beat the shortening, brown sugar, rice milk and vanilla in a mixer bowl at medium speed until blended. Beat in the Ener-G Egg Replacer mixture. Add the flour mixture and mix well. Stir in the carob chocolate chips.

Drop by tablespoonfuls 3 inches apart on nonstick cookie sheets.

Bake at 375 degrees for 9 to 10 minutes or until golden brown.

Yield: 3 dozen

DID YOU KNOW...
THAT THE LARGEST COOKIE EVER MADE WAS A CHOCOLATE CHIP COOKIE? IT HAD AN AREA OF 5,241.5 SQUARE FEET, A DIAMETER OF 81 FEET 8 INCHES, AND CONTAINED 2.8 TONS OF CHOCOLATE.

Cookie Pops
on a Stick

*2 cups (4 sticks) butter or
margarine, softened
1 teaspoon baking soda
2$\frac{1}{2}$ cups sugar
1 teaspoon extract flavor of choice
4$\frac{1}{2}$ cups self-rising flour
24 popsicle sticks
Sprinkles or other topping (optional)*

Beat the butter, baking soda, sugar
and extract in a mixer bowl until light
and fluffy. Beat in the flour.

Shape into balls using an ice cream
scoop. Press a popsicle stick into each
ball. Sprinkle the topping over the
cookies. Place on nonstick cookie
sheets. Press down on each cookie to
$\frac{1}{4}$-inch thickness, making sure that at
least 1 inch of the stick is covered
by the cookie.

Bake at 350 degrees for 15 minutes or
until the edges are light golden brown.

Yield: 2 dozen

Louie's Lemon
Cookies

*1 (2-layer) package lemon cake mix
2 eggs
$\frac{1}{3}$ cup vegetable oil
1 teaspoon lemon extract
Confectioners' sugar*

Combine the cake mix, eggs, oil and
lemon extract in a bowl and mix well.

Place confectioners' sugar in a bowl.
Drop the batter by teaspoonfuls into
the confectioners' sugar, rolling to coat.

Place on nonstick cookie sheets. Bake at
375 degrees for 6 to 9 minutes or until
the bottoms are light brown.

Yield: 2$\frac{1}{2}$ to 3$\frac{1}{2}$ dozen

No-Bake Cookies III

2 cups sugar
3 tablespoons baking cocoa
$\frac{1}{2}$ cup (1 stick) butter or margarine
$\frac{1}{2}$ cup milk
Dash of salt
3 cups quick-cooking oats
$\frac{1}{2}$ cup peanut butter
1 teaspoon vanilla extract

Combine the sugar, cocoa, butter, milk and salt in a saucepan. Bring to a rapid boil, stirring frequently. Boil for 1 minute.

Add the oats, peanut butter and vanilla and mix well. Drop by teaspoonfuls onto waxed paper immediately. Let stand until set.

Yield: 1 to 2 dozen

DID YOU KNOW...
THAT COCOA BEANS ARE FOUND IN THE PODS OR FRUIT OF THE COCOA TREE, AN EVERGREEN CULTIVATED MAINLY WITHIN 20 DEGREES OF THE EQUATOR? THEY ARE THE SOURCE OF ALL CHOCOLATE.

Pudding Cookies

³/₄ cup buttermilk baking mix
¹/₄ cup vegetable oil
1 egg
1 (4-ounce) package instant
pudding mix
¹/₂ cup chocolate chips
or nuts (optional)

Combine the baking mix, oil, egg and pudding mix in a bowl and mix well. Stir in the chocolate chips.

Drop by teaspoonfuls onto nonstick cookie sheets.

Bake at 350 degrees for 10 minutes or until a wooden pick inserted in the center comes out clean.

Yield: 1 to 2 dozen

Potato Chip Cookies

2 cups (4 sticks) butter or
margarine, softened
1¹/₂ cups sugar
2 teaspoons vanilla extract
2 eggs
3¹/₂ cups flour
1¹/₂ cups crushed potato chips

Cream the butter and sugar in a mixer bowl until light and fluffy. Beat in the vanilla and eggs. Add the flour and potato chips and mix well.

Drop by teaspoonfuls 2 inches apart onto lightly greased cookie sheets.

Bake at 350 degrees for 12 to 15 minutes.

Yield: 1 to 2 dozen

Oatmeal Carrot Bars

1/2 cup raisins
1 cup boiling water
1 cup whole wheat flour
1/2 cup quick-cooking oats
1 teaspoon baking powder
1/3 cup margarine, softened
1/2 cup packed light brown sugar
1 egg
1 1/4 cups grated carrots
1/2 teaspoon cinnamon
1/4 teaspoon nutmeg
1/2 teaspoon freshly grated lemon peel
1/2 teaspoon vanilla extract
1 tablespoon confectioners' sugar

Cover the raisins with the boiling water in a bowl. Soak for 15 minutes; drain and set aside.

Combine the flour, oats and baking powder in a bowl and mix well.

Cream the margarine and brown sugar in a large mixer bowl until light and fluffy. Beat in the egg. Stir in the carrots. Add the cinnamon, nutmeg and lemon peel and mix well. Add the flour mixture and beat until well blended. Add the vanilla and mix well. Stir in the raisins.

Spoon into a greased 9x13-inch baking pan. Bake at 350 degrees for 20 to 25 minutes or until browned. Cool completely.

Sprinkle with the confectioners' sugar. Cut into bars.

Yield: 2 dozen

Marshmallow Squares

¼ cup vegetable oil
4 ounces marshmallows
1 teaspoon vanilla extract
4 cups crisp rice cereal

Heat the oil in a large saucepan. Add the marshmallows. Cook over low heat until melted, stirring constantly. Stir in the vanilla. Add the cereal and mix well.

Spoon into a greased 8x8-inch baking pan and press down to pack. Cool.

Cut into squares.

Yield: 9 squares

Easy Peanut Brittle

2 cups shelled unsalted peanuts
2 cups sugar
½ teaspoon baking powder

Spread the peanuts over a lightly oiled baking sheet.

Cook the sugar in a heavy pan over low heat until melted and light brown, stirring constantly. Remove from the heat.

Stir in the baking powder just until blended. Pour immediately over the peanuts in a thin layer. Cool completely.

Break into pieces.

Yield: 1 pound

Rolled-on-the-Sidewalk Ice Cream

1 cup milk
1 cup whipping cream
¼ cup pasteurized egg product
½ cup sugar
½ teaspoon vanilla extract
Fruit or nuts (optional)
Crushed ice
¾ cup (or more) rock salt

Combine the milk, cream, pasteurized egg product, sugar and vanilla in a bowl and mix well. Stir in the fruit. Pour into a clean 1-pound coffee can with a tight-fitting lid; cover. Place inside a clean 3-pound coffee can with a tight-fitting lid. Fill the larger can with crushed ice, packing well around the small can. Sprinkle with ¾ cup rock salt. Cover the larger can.

Roll back and forth on the sidewalk for 10 minutes.

Remove the smaller can from the larger can. Stir the ice cream with a spatula, scraping the side of the can.

Replace the small can inside the larger can, adding crushed ice and rock salt as needed.

Roll for 5 minutes longer.

Yield: 6 servings

Substitutions for Common Allergenic Foods

Fortunately, there are many substitutes for the foods previously listed to which people are most often allergic. Most substitutes are readily available so there is no excuse for not using them when you do react to one of the other foods.

Wheat Substitutes

1 cup wheat flour equals:

$^2/_3$ cup oat flour

$1^1/_3$ cups rolled oats

$1^1/_4$ cups rye flour

1 cup rye meal

$^7/_8$ cup rice flour

$^5/_8$ cup potato starch flour

$^3/_4$ cup cornmeal

$^3/_4$ cup soy flour

$^1/_2$ cup barley flour

$^1/_3$ cup potato flour and $^5/_8$ cup rice flour

$^1/_2$ cup potato flour and $^1/_2$ cup rye flour

Note: When cooking with one of these flours, cook at lower temperatures for a longer time. The end products from baking with these flours tend to be crustier and crumblier.

For making sauces and gravies, 1 tablespoon wheat flour equals:

2 teaspoons quick tapioca

$^1/_2$ tablespoon arrowroot

$^1/_2$ tablespoon rice flour

Egg Substitutes

One egg equals:

1) 2 tablespoons water + 1 tablespoon oil + 2 tablespoons baking powder
2) 2 tablespoons water + 2 teaspoons baking powder
3) 1 tablespoon ground flax + 3 tablespoons water
4) 2 tablespoons liquid + 2 tablespoons flour + $^1/_2$ tablespoon fat + $^1/_2$ teaspoon baking powder

Milk Substitutes

Nut Milks

$^3/_4$ cup raw almonds, sesame seeds or walnuts

$3^1/_2$ cups water

2 tablespoons honey

1 teaspoon vanilla extract

Blend nuts or seeds at high speed in blender until a fine meal is produced. Add water and blend until smooth. Then add honey and vanilla and blend for 30 seconds. Store in refrigerator. Yield: 1 quart

Note: Do not give honey to children under one year of age, due to chance of botulism poisoning.

Where to Purchase
Foods for Allergy Diets

The following are selected sources of foods for allergy diets. In part, this list is intended to convey the message that diet foods are readily available. A listing here is not an endorsement of the products or stores. Also check health and ethnic food stores, and ethnic sections of grocery stores.

Beechnut Baby Foods Co.
605 Third Ave., New York, NY 10016
Professional and consumer services. Wheat, egg, milk, gluten, and citrus-free products

Chicago Dietetic Supply, Inc.
Sales Dept., 405 East Shawmut Ave., P.O. Box 529, LaGrange, IL 60525
Milk, wheat, rye, oat, corn, gluten, and grain-free products

Ener-G Foods
P.O. Box 84487, Seattle, WA 98121
Gluten, and wheat-free products; egg and milk substitutes

Fearn Soya Foods
1206 North 31st Avenue, Melrose Park, IL 60160
Milk-free and wheat-free products

General Mills
Nutritional Service, Dept. 5, 9200 Wayzata Blvd., Minneapolis, MN 55440
Cereal for hypo-allergenic diets in grain sensitivity. Also Dietetic Paygel-P low-gluten recipes

Gerber Baby Foods Company
Fremont, MI 49412
Egg, milk, wheat, citrus, gluten, and corn-free products

Giusto Speciality Foods, Inc.
420 Fulton St., San Francisco, CA 94102
Rice bread mix, lima-potato bread mix, and lima-soybean mix

Kanana Banana Flakes
Available at drug and grocery stores
Egg, wheat, and milk-free

Loma Linda Foods
Riverside, CA 92505

Special Foods
9207 Shotgun Court, Springfield, VA 22150

N.E.E.D.S. Home Shopping Service
609 Nottingham Road, Syracuse, NY 13244

Contributors

Joey Bartelson
Katie Bartelson
Kelly Collins
Matthew Collins
Nicole Collins
Anne Loranger
Kayleigh Loranger
Philip Loranger
Danny MacIsaac
Jacob MacIsaac
Elena Macrelli
Ellen Macrelli

Hillary Macrelli
Maria "Dolly" Macrelli
Matthew Macrelli
Robert Macrelli
Chris Peterson
Pat Peterson
Sharon Peterson
Denise Robbins
Eugene Vega
Mary Volpe
Claire Wilson, M.D.

About the Photographer

Robin Agostini lives in Littleton, Massachusetts, with her husband and daughter. She has been interested in photography since her early teens. She has done several weddings for friends and has been doing children's pictures for the past few years. Recently, she has begun reproducing and altering existing pictures, using computer software to combine two or more pictures as was done for the Macrelli family photograph used in this book.

Robin Agostini
117 New Estate Road
Littleton, Massachusetts 01460

Credits

Nutritional Advisor: Becky Bradley, MS, RD, CDE
Legal Advisor: Eve Horwitz
David's Fund Logo Design: James Millerick

About the Artist

Linda Zebrowski lives in the Boston area with her daughter and son. Some of her works, miniature sculptures, are on display at the Constitution Museum in Charlestown, Massachusetts.

Linda Zebrowski
P.O. Box 233
Reading, Massachusetts 01867

References

Chalmers, Irena. 1994. T*he Great Food Almanac.* San Francisco: Collins Publishers.

Hendrickson, Robert. 1997. *QPB Encyclopedia of Word and Phrase Origins.* New York: Facts on File, Inc.

Herbst, Sharon Tyler. 1995. *Food Lover's Companion.* Second Edition. Hauppauge, New York: Barron's Educational Services, Inc.

Lockwood, Georgene. 1998. *The Complete Idiot's Guide to Crafts with Kids.* New York, New York: Alpha Books.

Trotter, Charlie, Judi Carle and Sari Zernich. 1997. *Gourmet Cooking for Dummies.* Foster City, Calif.: IDG Books Worldwide, Inc.

Children's Illustrated Encyclopedia. 1998. New York: DK Publishing Inc.

The Guinness Book of World Records. Edited by Mark C. Young. 1997. Stamford, Conn.: Guinness Publishing Ltd.

Index

Cooking Under the
Rainbow

Lahey Clinic
Philanthropy
41 Mall Road
Burlington, Massachusetts
01805-0105

Please send _____ copies of **Cooking Under the Rainbow**

$14.95 each $ _____

Postage and Handling $4.00 each $ _____

TOTAL $ _____

Name _____

Street Address _____

City _____ State _____ Zip _____

Telephone _____

Method of Payment: [   ] VISA   [   ] MasterCard   [   ] American Express
[   ] Check payable to "Cooking Under the Rainbow"

Account Number _____ Expiration Date _____

Signature _____

Photocopies will be accepted.